Original title:
The Porch of Solitude

Copyright © 2025 Creative Arts Management OÜ
All rights reserved.

Author: Victor Mercer
ISBN HARDBACK: 978-1-80587-176-7
ISBN PAPERBACK: 978-1-80587-646-5

A Solace Found in Silence

In my own little space, oh so neat,
The cat's found a chair, can't find my seat.
With socks on my hands and tea on my nose,
I ponder the highs and the lows of my toes.

Birds chirp gossip, the news of the day,
While squirrels plot heists in a sneaky ballet.
The world spins outside, it's a hilarious race,
Yet all I need's laughter in this cozy place.

The Evening Calls for Solitude

The sun dips low, a cheeky orange ball,
I'm here with my snacks, ready to sprawl.
Reluctant to leave this snug, silly lair,
I debate with my fridge – we're quite the pair!

Breezes mess my hair, a relentless tease,
I chuckle at clouds; they float with such ease.
The world is a circus, an all-time low,
Yet here I find joy, just watching the show.

Nature's Canvas of Quietude

The trees tell tales, their leaves seem to giggle,
I swear one just winked – it gave me a riddle.
Flowers wear hats, quite fancy and bright,
While ants carry crumbs like a feast for the night.

Bugs boogie along a swift, breezy tune,
I dance with my shadow, a silly cartoon.
Oh, nature, you trickster, you color my day,
In a world full of chuckles, I'm here to stay.

Serenity Wrapped in Twilight

As dusk settles in, I'm laced with delight,
With one eye on the stars, it's a comical sight.
Fireflies flicker, like tiny disco balls,
Making me smile at their whimsical calls.

The nighttime's a show, bright and absurd,
I guess even crickets have wisdom unheard.
Wrapped up in this calm, oh what a fun ride,
In the humor of night, I'll happily bide.

Whispers of a Quiet Evening

The crickets sing a silly tune,
While I hum along with my old raccoon.
An owl hoots loud, thinks he's so wise,
But can't find his way, oh what a surprise!

The breeze carries whispers, soft and light,
As squirrels debate if it's day or night.
A moth flutters by, thinks it's a star,
But it just flew too close to my candy jar!

Shadows Beneath the Canopy

Under the trees, shadows dance and play,
A raccoon sneaks snacks, thinking it's his day.
The branches gossip, slapping the air,
While I sip lemonade, without a care.

A branch falls down, with a thud and a plop,
I jump like a kid, almost spill my drop.
But laughter erupts from the grass at my feet,
As a beetle rolls by, thinking he's neat!

Solitary Steps on Weathered Wood

Each creak of the boards like a song in disguise,
Maybe the wood just wants to express its sighs.
I tiptoe around like a stealthy old cat,
Tripping over thoughts and my old straw hat.

The sunbeams tickle, making me grin,
As ants march by, planning their din.
The swing sways gently, like it's trying to tease,
Whispering jokes to the buzzing bees!

Echoes of a Forgotten Day

A day once bright now wrapped in dusk,
The shadows chuckle, it's all very brusque.
The wind tells secrets, or maybe just lies,
While frogs compete in a chorus of sighs.

I sit and ponder this whimsical scene,
As a cat steals my chair, feeling so queen.
The sun bows out, with a wink and a cheer,
Leaving me here, sipping lemonade and beer!

A Chair for One

A chair sits proudly on the plank,
With snack crumbs scattered like a prank.
It creaks and groans, a friendly plea,
'Come sit with me, just you and me!'

The sunlight dances, shadows sway,
While squirrels plot their daring play.
An empty cup, my silent mate,
We're a duo, both out of fate.

I tell the chair all my wild schemes,
It listens close, though it just beams.
My coffee spills, my thoughts take flight,
Is it me or is this chair too tight?

With laughter echoing all around,
The solitude we've tightly found.
A single chair, a world so wide,
With every joke, my grin won't hide.

Moments Wrapped in Solitude

They say that quiet breeds the best,
But I find that's a funny jest.
A mouse skitters, a cat takes chase,
In solitude, I lose the race!

My thoughts parade in silly lines,
Like socks that lose their paired designs.
Each moment here, a circus act,
In solitude, my mind distracts.

A bird alights, gives me a wink,
As I decide to pour a drink.
It laughs at me, the little fool,
In moments wrapped, I drop my cool.

With bursting giggles, I sit still,
The days go by, a carefree thrill.
In quietude, the giggles grow,
Wrapped in thoughts, a funny show.

Breeze-kissed Thoughts

Whispers of wind like tickling hands,
Playfully teasing through empty lands.
My thoughts take flight like paper planes,
Breeze-kissed musings that never wane.

A butterfly laughs, flits in and out,
While I ponder why I'm here, no doubt.
My chair's a throne of great delight,
In solitude, it feels just right.

The sun peeks in as if to say,
These thoughts of mine are here to stay!
I chuckle at clouds, oh, what a sight,
Breezes dance while my mind takes flight.

With every gust, a giggle grows,
In the stillness, joy overflows.
My thoughts, like bubbles, rise and roam,
In this funny space, I find my home.

The Stillness Between Heartbeats

In the quiet gaps where whispers fade,
I watch the ants in their grand parade.
They carry crumbs like weights of gold,
In stillness, stories beg to be told.

I time my breath, a playful game,
The heartbeat skips, it's never the same.
In these moments, I strike a pose,
Like a statue but with funny toes.

The laughter echoes in my mind,
While I search for a seat to find.
A chair that wiggles, an odd ballet,
In the stillness, I sway and sway.

With giggles hiding behind closed doors,
I ponder those unsung little chores.
In the space between each heartbeat's tick,
Solitude dresses me in jokes so thick.

Fading Light and Mellow Moods

In the twilight, shadows dance,
Chasing squirrels at a glance.
Three old chairs, a game of jive,
Who knew they'd be so alive?

A cat performs a clumsy leap,
While the crickets start to creep.
With one ear up, and one ear down,
She plots to catch a wayward clown.

The wind whispers secrets low,
As laughter drifts, soft and slow.
An ant parade, oh what a sight,
Marching home, in fading light.

And as the evening hums along,
We sing off-key, our favorite song.
Joy in stillness, absurd delight,
Who knew solitude could feel so bright?

Moments Held in Still Air

Sitting here with nothing to do,
Even the flies seem askew.
A shadow from the tree does tease,
Urging me to fold my knees.

The sky pulls a sunset stunt,
While I ponder the ant's last hunt.
Do they know their grand design?
Or is their quest just for a dine?

The wind makes faces with the leaves,
Hiding laughter up its sleeves.
A breeze that suggests wise old tales,
But really just tickles my nails.

In this whimsy, I find my bliss,
Mirthful moments I can kiss.
Why rush through life, let time unfurl,
When humor swirls in a steady whirl?

The Calm Before the Nightfall

A lantern flickers, calls for cheer,
Yet here I sit with a glass of beer.
The night owl hoots, "What's the fuss?"
I say, "Just don't make a fuss!"

A tumbleweed rolls by with style,
Who knew that grass could be so vile?
The corner cats gather for the show,
In silent agreement on their woe.

The sun dips low, like a shy friend,
Leaving just enough for lights to blend.
Crickets chirp, they missed the cue,
As fireflies pop in for a view.

So here I ponder, sip and smile,
With creatures plotting in this while.
Before the dark, a chuckle's call,
Life's quiet jests can thrill us all.

Mindful Breath in Dusk's Glow

With the day's laughter softening,
Even the sun seems to be coughing.
A ticklish breeze whirls by my ear,
"Hey buddy, did you lose something here?"

I pet the bench, it's like Old Sam,
Witty and wise, a real dear friend.
We share a wink as the cool night calls,
Chasing shadows, avoiding falls.

The moon peeks in with a playful grin,
While twinkling stars join in the spin.
They tease and joke, a cosmic laugh,
As planets glide on their own path.

In this moment, all is swell,
Nature's humor, I know it well.
So raise a toast to the quiet night,
In silly peace, life feels just right!

When the World Retreats

In my chair, I sit and sigh,
A squirrel steals my snack, oh my!
The world can buzz, let chaos bloom,
I chuckle as I find more room.

Birds debate atop the fence,
They squabble loud, it makes no sense.
I sip my tea, and catch their show,
What joy it brings, this one-man show.

The sun dips low, a gentle tease,
The leaves giggle in the breeze.
I wave goodbye to the day's fuss,
Embracing silence, just me and us.

The moon joins in with a bright wink,
As I ponder how to rethink.
With laughter echoing through the night,
I find my peace in this delight.

The Calm Before Tomorrow's Dawn

Awaiting dawn with pillow fights,
While shadows dance with silly bites.
The clock ticks slow, my eyelids drop,
A battle won, it's time to flop.

Cats plot mischief on the floor,
While crickets play a symphony score.
I stretch my limbs, a yawning spree,
Planning schemes with a soft chuckle, whee!

The light creeps in, an orange tease,
I wonder if I should get up, please.
But oh, this bed, it's just too snug,
I resign again, a cozy hug.

Laughter lingers, dreams take flight,
A world of fun before the light.
Tomorrow waits with all its plans,
But here I bask in silliness' hands.

Starlit Reverie in Solace's Arms

Stars wink down, a glimmering tease,
I giggle softly, lost in the breeze.
A raccoon dances, oh what a sight,
I cheer him on, my heart feels light.

The night hums low, a playful tone,
While shadows flit, I feel at home.
In the calm of dusk, weird thoughts arise,
About who eats first, me or the fries?

Fireflies join in with flickering fun,
Chasing their tails, they surely run.
I clap and laugh at the cheeky game,
Life's silly moments, never the same.

With every flicker, whispers of glee,
Thanking the cosmos for letting me be.
As stars take their bows, I rise and spin,
In this quiet place, where laughter begins.

A Tapestry of Quiet Moments

In the gentle shade, I weave my dreams,
With threads of laughter and complicated schemes.
A breeze brings giggles from the nearby trees,
As I ponder life's mysteries over my peas.

The world outside plays its frantic game,
While I lounge here, feeling quite the same.
A lizard slides by, looking bemused,
While I salute him, giggling, confused.

Time stands still as shadows stretch long,
I hum a tune, a definitely wrong song.
With every pause, I hear the whimsy,
Of ordinary life, making me frisky.

Sundown wraps me in a gentle hug,
As I finish my snack, a jelly slug.
Moments like these, crafty and bright,
Are where I find joy, pure and light.

Tea and Time in Stillness

A cup of brew, I take my seat,
The clock ticks slow with gentle beat.
My cat's a judge, with regal flair,
He sips my thoughts, as I just stare.

The kettle whistles, sings its tune,
While I debate with moths at noon.
They dance around, their wings so spry,
And swear they're learning how to fly.

A biscuit crumbles, crumbs take flight,
While laughter echoes in soft light.
Each sip is filled with comic grace,
As I imagine a tea-filled race.

But time drips slow, oh what a tease,
I sip my drink, the world at ease.
With every gulp, my giggles rise,
As moths compose their own reprise.

Beneath the Gaze of the Stars

At night I sit, my drink in hand,
The sky's a canvas, oh so grand.
I speak to stars, they giggle back,
In twinkling jokes, my heart they crack.

A meteor whizzes, "Catch me quick!"
I laugh and shout, "You're quite the trick!"
They wink and nod, a cosmic jest,
While I recline, and feel so blessed.

The clouds are sheep, they float and roam,
I ask them kindly, "Where's your home?"
They laugh, reply, "We follow dreams!"
And drift away in moonlit beams.

With every sip, my thoughts take flight,
The universe is pure delight.
I toast the night, a saucy cheer,
With winks and grins, my stars draw near.

Hushed Conversations with the Moon

A silver orb hangs in the night,
I chat away with wit, not fright.
She listens close, our secrets share,
While crickets serenade the air.

"Why so blue?" I tease her glance,
She lights up bright, "Let's dance, let's prance!"
With each soft word, her shadows play,
We giggle softly, in the sway.

Her glow, a laugh that bends the trees,
With light so sweet, it's like a breeze.
I tell her tales of silly things,
Of frogs that wear most funny rings.

In quiet chuckles, time slips by,
With every laugh, we touch the sky.
The world below, a quiet dream,
As night wraps us in joy's soft beam.

Raindrops on Weathered Planks

The rain drops dance upon the wood,
Creating rhythms that feel so good.
I watch them juggle, bubble, splash,
As puddles form, I can't help but laugh.

With tiny taps, the raindrops play,
They bring the sunflowers out to sway.
"Hey, you there!" I call to a drip,
"Don't slip away, come join my trip!"

Each patter tells a joke so sly,
The trees lean in, they must comply.
While squirrels take covers, that's a feat,
As raindrops tumble like sprightly feet.

Then lightning flashes, thunder roars,
I grin and shout, "Again, encore!"
The weather's wacky, but so divine,
With every drop, I toast with wine.

A Journey Within Stillness

In a chair that creaks and sways,
The cat keeps watch in lazy ways.
I sip my tea, it's quite a feat,
Deciding whether to nap or eat.

The world outside throws fits and feuds,
While I ponder life with silly moods.
Should I dance? Nah, just one more peek,
At squirrels debating their next cheeky tweak.

As shadows stretch and dusk draws near,
I chuckle at my thoughts, oh dear!
I wrote a novel, or so I claim,
But all that's left is a doodle of shame.

So here I sit with humorous grace,
My mind a cluttered, joyful space.
When asked for wisdom, I just shrug,
And sip again from my cozy mug.

Solitary Breath of Evening

Evening steals in with giggly lights,
It brings the chorus of fuzzy sights.
I chase fireflies, a silly quest,
For peace of mind in their strange jest.

There's a box of snacks, my trusty loot,
A cookie here, and there's a fruit.
But oh, they whisper, 'Share with us!'
As crumbs rain down, that's quite a fuss!

I find it funny, this quiet place,
Where thoughts outwit at their own pace.
The breeze carries whispers, a gentle tease,
While I pretend to be at ease.

And as stars blink in their nightly show,
I laugh at how little I seem to know.
A sage of snacks, a master recluse,
Yet in the stillness, I let my heart loose.

Tales Carried by the Wind

A breeze arrives with secrets to tell,
Of mischief danced by a pesky bell.
I grab my hat, it flaps like mad,
In this comedic war with the latest fad.

Neighbors grumble, here comes that gust,
Whipping around like it's been thrust.
It plays with leaves, a playful clown,
As I sit and giggle in my old gown.

The night spills stories, whistling loud,
Each crack in the darkness, a quirky crowd.
My thoughts take flight, sharing cheeky grins,
While laughter rises as joy begins.

Alone but not lonely, the wind's my friend,
With absurd plots it loves to send.
In this quirky twilight, a gentle spin,
I revel in chaos, let the tales begin.

Glimpses Through the Veil of Night

Under a moon that winks so bright,
I peer through shadows, a curious sight.
A raccoon's party, oh what a sham,
They're serving snacks from my trash can!

I chuckle softly, with fingers crossed,
As they dance around, their foam hats tossed.
The stars blink down, amused and wise,
While I sip my cocoa and roll my eyes.

Night holds laughter in its soft embrace,
With creatures plotting in this wild space.
Each soft rustle a giggling delight,
In this quirky world bathed in moonlight.

So let the night sweep me into dreams,
Where nothing's ever quite as it seems.
I'll snicker at life, its zany delight,
As I drift through the veil of the starry night.

Unseen Threads of Contemplation

In a chair that creaks with glee,
Thoughts wander loose and free.
The cat sits plotting by my feet,
Kicky paw and whiskers sweet.

Sipping tea in half a dream,
Staring at the fence's seam.
A squirrel scolds with raucous flair,
As I pretend that I don't care.

The sun dips low, the shadows prance,
A crabby mood is gone by chance.
I question life, the moon, the stars,
With no one here to stop my bars.

A bird that chirps a mock romance,
Is sent to give my mind a dance.
While laughter echoes through the breeze,
All alone, yet feeling pleased.

Melodies of the Nightingale

Upon the porch as twilight falls,
I serenade the painted walls.
The neighbor's dog joins in the throng,
A off-key bark, a quirky song.

With crickets playing hidden tunes,
And fireflies wearing tiny moons.
I wave to shadows down the lane,
Conversations with the night, mundane.

A pizza slice becomes a muse,
As laughter spills, I start to snooze.
The chair rocks gently, time unwinds,
Dreaming of singsong, rhymes, and blinds.

Yet time's a thief, it likes to creep,
In this calm, I thought to sleep.
What should be wise turns slightly wild,
As dawn arrives, I'm still a child.

Footprints of Forgotten Conversations

In the stillness, echoes dare,
Whispers float through evening air.
I talk to bugs, they seem to care,
Their tiny eyes like jewels stare.

Memories dance on creaky floors,
Conversations blend like soft snores.
A breeze confesses secrets grand,
To blades of grass and grains of sand.

The moon responds with nods and winks,
To all my wild and silly blinks.
A sage old tree leans in to hear,
My tales of life, both bold and queer.

As laughter bubbles in the night,
Forgotten voices take their flight.
Each step I take on this worn stage,
Leaves imprints of my silly age.

The Lullaby of Dusk

The day retreats, a funny sight,
Hiccups in the fading light.
I sing to stars, they roll their eyes,
As twilight hums its soft goodbyes.

Mosquitoes buzz in podcast tones,
Complaining loudly from their thrones.
A sneeze escapes, it breaks the calm,
As crickets play a lilting psalm.

Hmm, lullabies to empty chairs,
Invite the world to share its cares.
I chuckle softly, ghosts in tow,
They dance around, they steal the show.

With giggles trapped in evening's grasp,
The moonlight grips my thoughts, a clasp.
As slumber drapes its gentle shawl,
I whisper dreams, they catch, they fall.

A Retreat for Weary Souls

In the corner, a chair awaits,
Where laughter lingers, time abates.
A cat sprawls wide, blocking the sun,
While I sip tea, avoiding the run.

Jokes float by like clouds in the sky,
Each hour drags like a snail on the fly.
With snacks on the table, crumbs in my hair,
Naps are the secret—the favorite affair.

The wind hums a tune, a silly old song,
I can't help but hum it; oh, what's gone wrong?
Frogs are my critics, croaking away,
As I tap my foot to their froggy ballet.

Breeze plays a prank, making leaves dance,
A moment of bliss, could this be chance?
With every tick-tock, my heart feels so free,
In this quirky retreat, just my snacks and me.

Solitary Reflections on a Lazy Afternoon

Sipping my drink while the world goes by,
Sunshine rays make me sigh and comply.
Birds gossip loudly, sharing their tales,
While I stretch and yawn; oh, life never fails!

A squirrel hops close, eyeing my snack,
But I give him a glare; he scuttles back.
It's a standoff now, who will win here?
My treasures are safe—I settle with cheer.

Clouds drift in patterns, a comedy show,
One looks like a cake, but no! It's a crow.
I chuckle and smile, feeling so grand,
While time slips away like grains from my hand.

A nap beckons me; I close my eyes tight,
In dreams I am soaring, oh, what a sight!
But first, one more cookie, let's savor the last,
As the afternoon fades; oh, how time has passed.

Resting in the Embrace of Dusk

As evening creeps in, I lounge with delight,
The sky wears a gown stitched with pink and white.
Fireflies flicker like tiny lost stars,
If only they didn't crash into my jars!

A sip of my drink; it's almost too sweet,
Like a prankster's best work, a bad treat.
The crickets are playing their evening jam,
While I join the chorus; oh, how they scram!

Neighbors shout jokes that echo with glee,
I chuckle along; who can disagree?
With shadows that stretch like silly old cats,
We dance in the moonlight, all wearing hats.

The stars start to wink, and I wave back too,
Is it normal to chat with a shoe?
Embraced by dusk, my heart's in a spin,
In this funny twilight, where nonsense begins.

Echoes of Solitude at Sundown

As the sun takes a bow, I wave from my chair,
Content in my bubble, without a care.
A raccoon strolls by, with swagger and flair,
Must think it's a star; oh, can you compare?

The swing starts to creak, like it knows a joke,
It chuckles out loud with every lil' poke.
I laugh at the moon, who's turning so shy,
It paints the night sky while the day waves goodbye.

Stars join the melee, twinkling with sass,
Their gossip in whispers—a nocturnal pass.
I toss them my wishes, they giggle delight,
As crickets provide the most comical fright.

With shadows aplenty, my spirit takes flight,
In this echo of giggles, all feels just right.
So here's to the silence, wrapped in pure fun,
With laughter and starlight, the day's finally done.

A Retreat from the Clamor

In a chair that wobbles, I sit and sway,
Watching squirrels plot their grand ballet.
The neighbors yell, their garden's alive,
While I sip my drink, feeling carefree and jive.

A honeybee buzzes, a playful dance,
Trying to steal my sugary chance.
The dog next door thinks he's a great wolf,
As he barks at shadows with rights to the gulf.

The cat takes the sun, stretched out like a rug,
Giving me side-eye for another mug.
I ponder my snacks, a perfect delight,
As the world spins on, I'm out of the fight.

The trees whisper secrets, their leaves all a-quake,
While I worry about the next slice of cake.
The world rushes past, but here I remain,
In my blissful cocoon, where laughter's the gain.

Secrets Shared with Lonesome Skies

The clouds float by with a giggle or two,
Mocking the sun as it tries to break through.
Birds gossip loudly, squawking and shrill,
While I snicker softly, sipping my dill.

Lonely winds chat with an old wooden fence,
Whispering tales of friendship immense.
The trees laugh with me, their branches a mess,
As the world just rushes, in constant distress.

A rogue raccoon might join in my fun,
Stealing away treasures, thinking he's won.
I throw him a nibble, a bribe for a joke,
As the sky holds its breath, hoping I'll poke.

The neighbor's cat saunters, all of a strut,
Pretending to care, with a flick of her gut.
Yet in this moment, with skies so sincere,
I share my confessions, with giggles and cheer.

The Language of Raindrops

Raindrops tap dance on my tin roof,
Each one a chuckle, a little goof.
They splatter and scatter, a splashy affair,
Making jokes of puddles, without a care.

A worm spins tales in the cool, wet ground,
While I chuckle softly at the splashy sound.
The drip from the eaves plays symphonic tones,
As the sky throws a fit with its murmurs and moans.

My slippers are soggy, my hair's gone awry,
But I'm fit to play, with a grin and a sigh.
Jumping in puddles, I forget all the drear,
For raindrops are laughter, so loud and so clear.

The sun peeks through, but don't be misled,
It just wants to warm up what rain has said.
So I'll dance in the drizzles, with joy and some flair,
In a world where the weather is never a bear.

Sighs of a Fading Day

The sun yawns big, as it dips low,
Painting the skies in a glorious show.
Fireflies blink in a blinking spree,
While crickets prepare their night symphony.

Chairs creak softly with every deep breath,
As the day stretches, feeling quite heft.
I sip on my tea, watching shadows play,
And chuckle at all of the silliness today.

A cow in the field looks lost in thought,
As if pondering why it's all for naught.
The moon grins shyly, coming out for a peek,
While frogs croak out sonnets, each one unique.

So here in the twilight, I find my own way,
Laughing at life as it wanes toward gray.
With each fading moment, a smirk must suffice,
For laughter, my friend, is the best kind of vice.

As Shadows Merge and Part

When evening whispers to the trees,
The dog claims my chair with a sneeze.
The cat rolls over, just out of reach,
While I ponder life lessons from a peach.

Friends call me, their laughter clear,
"Join us outside for some cold beer!"
But here I sit, in cool dusk's glow,
With my snacks arranged in a neat little row.

I watch the shadows bend and twist,
They have their own party — I can't resist!
A game of tag on the chipped wood floor,
While I chuckle and pray for just one encore!

As night melds laughter with a sigh,
I expect my chair to soon fly high.
Yet here I reign, in my quirky throne,
Blessed by solitude and my dog's happy groan.

Crickets Serenade the Stillness

Crickets chirp a silly tune,
While I munch on leftover prune.
The stars blink down with mischief's gleam,
As I wonder if I'm in a dream.

A squirrel scolds me for being still,
Telling me I need more thrill.
But how can I, with such a feast,
In my quiet hunt for the perfect beast?

The moon tries dancing, twinkling along,
But trips on shadows with a fateful bong.
While I laugh quietly, caught in this spell,
Wondering if I have a story to tell.

So let the night unfurl its jest,
With crickets playing their very best.
Here's to laughter, snacks, and stars,
In a little slice of life that's absurdly ours!

Embracing the Quiet

Settled snugly with my cup of tea,
I hear the peeps of a neighbor's bee.
They wave hello from their annoying hum,
I return with a silent, peaceful thrum.

Squirrels scamper, playing hide and seek,
While I debate if I'd prefer a leak.
The neighbors argue over whose lawn is best,
I sit back, here enjoying my quest.

Each heartbeat echoes like a soft old drum,
What fun it is, I admit—I'm numb!
But who needs noise when I have this bliss?
Each sound that flutters is one I won't miss.

So I sip my tea, envisioning grand plans,
While plotting where to store my exam cans.
This stillness calls in a funny kind of way,
Embracing the quiet saves all my day!

The Auras of Day's End

As sunlight dips, colors burst and twirl,
The sky paints scenes, a whimsical swirl.
The clouds compete with a silly fight,
Throwing shades of pink, red, and light.

My sandals are missing, who knows where?
While my feet cheer for freedom, they're a little bare!
The wind joins in with a breezy dance,
Whispering secrets—should I take a chance?

A frog leaps up, ready for a chat,
Proclaims loudly, "I'm quite the acrobat!"
As I chuckle, he hops, hops away,
Perhaps tomorrow he'll play a new play.

With twilight glowing, laughter rings true,
This evening of chaos feels totally new.
I sigh with joy, a soft little wink,
Embracing the silliness while I think!

Lanterns of Loneliness

A single light bulb swings high,
A moth dances like it's shy.
I sit here with my cup of tea,
Wondering if the neighbors see.

The cat stares at shadows on the floor,
While I contemplate who comes through my door.
Is it too late to call for a snack?
Oh wait, it's just the sound of my own back.

A squirrel giggles, wearing a crown,
As I try to make sense of this town.
Do they hear my thoughts, these trees?
Or is the wind just trying to tease?

So here I sit in my comfy chair,
Talking to cushions, pouring out air.
If solitude's funny, then I'm the jester,
In this grand show, I'm the lone investor.

Constellations of Contemplation

Stars above blink with a jest,
As I ponder if this is the best.
Should I dance or just sit tight?
The crickets laugh under moonlight.

A thought pops like a bubblegum dream,
Would I look silly in a bright green beam?
Or do my pajamas still make me look cool?
In the grand universe, who's the fool?

My chair's creaking like a wise old sage,
While I scribble thoughts on a napkin page.
Do I wish for company's delightful sound,
Or is my own voice the best around?

The wind shares secrets, or so it seems,
As I muse over my wildest dreams.
If laughter's the answer, I'll never know,
But at least my imagination gets to flow!

Emptiness Filled with Stars

An empty space, just me and my tea,
The stars above giggle, 'Look at he!'
An echo resounds, or could it be me?
I swear I heard laughter among the leaves.

The porch swing creaks like it's got a joke,
A ticking clock's my only bloke.
It tells me to hurry, don't sit so still,
But how can I rush this glorious thrill?

A gust of wind plays tag with my hat,
And I chuckle at it, 'Come back, come back!'
I never thought solitude could be this fun,
Oh, how I love this solo run.

The stars rolling in their endless dance,
They wink at me, urging a chance.
In this cosmic bubble, silly and shy,
I realize laughter is never awry.

Gentle Waves of Nostalgia

Sitting here, the waves gently sway,
They whisper secrets of yesterday.
I giggle at the past, it feels so near,
As seagulls squawk and make it clear.

A bottle floats by, full of lost notes,
Wishing it carried my old love quotes.
But here I chuckle, made of sand and sun,
These memories are nice, but not much fun.

The breeze brings tales of laughter and tears,
Reminding me softly of forgotten years.
Did I really wear socks with my flip-flops?
Oh, nostalgia's waves never truly stop!

With the tide slipping back into the sea,
I ponder a world that's just for me.
If my laughter rides waves, I'll let it fly,
In this gentle chaos, I'll just ride high.

Portraits of Unspoken Thoughts

On a seat made for one, I sit,
Where squirrels plan their next big hit.
The world spins fast, but here it slows,
While I ponder why my coffee glows.

Neighbors chat about their cats,
While I debate with my old hats.
They say silence is golden, I beg to differ,
Mine just makes my thoughts get stiffer.

I wave at clouds as if they care,
In my mind, we're quite the pair.
Oh look, a butterfly with a hat!
Is this what life is with a spat?

A bird steals crumbs from my snack,
Critiques my style, as if on track.
But here I laugh at thought's wild race,
In this chair, I've found my place.

Solitude's Soft Footfall

On my step, the world's a joke,
A hawk once sniffed, but now it pokes.
I chat with shadows, bold and bright,
While they plot my next midnight fright.

The flowers nod as I share my woes,
They whisper back in a language of foes.
A passing car plays a tune so lame,
In the game of life, I'm just a name.

The wind tells tales of lost socks,
As I sip tea in mismatched frocks.
Laughter can be heard in stretches wide,
While I check for crumbs I try to hide.

Invisible friends, they laugh and sing,
Bringing joy to this odd little thing.
In this stillness, I find my cheer,
With witty banter and no one near.

Serenity's Refuge in Noise

In a whirlwind of chatter, I gleam,
Finding solace in a daydream.
The cats of the street take a charming stroll,
As I question if they have a goal.

Breezes bump into my quietude,
While I sip lemonade, seeking mood.
A ladybird looks for a cozy nook,
But my arm's just a good spot to cook!

Sounds of laughter drift from afar,
It sounds like someone's chasing a car.
A kid with a kite, in a whimsical race,
While I chuckle at the joy on his face.

The noise wraps around like an old friend,
Bringing mess and chaos that won't end.
Yet here I sit in my cozy nook,
With whispers and giggles, and more to book.

The Glimmer of a Forgotten Dream

In a chair that squeaks like a broken toot,
I ponder where my lost dreams hoot.
With frogs on a quest to croak their best,
While I search for memories at their quest.

The sun winks at me through leafy shades,
And I giggle at life's quirky parades.
Clouds like marshmallows float on by,
As I wonder if they'd like to fly.

A breeze frolics with my hair so wild,
And whispers secrets like a playful child.
In this moment of whimsy and cheer,
I chase a glimmer that vanishes near.

Tickles of laughter echo around,
Even the ants seem joyfully profound.
Here in this space, without a dream's fright,
I'm nestled in funny, oh what a sight!

Embrace of the Hushed Hour

In the quiet hour, I sit and stare,
A squirrel's grand heist, a nut, a dare.
I sip my tea, oh what a sight,
A dance of shadows, a playful light.

The wind whispers secrets, I can't quite hear,
My slippers squeak, it brings me cheer.
With every thought, my mind takes flight,
What if my cat could teach me to write?

The neighbor's dog howls, oh what a tune,
Could he join my band, beneath the moon?
I clap my hands, we'll start a show,
Unsanctioned music, in the fading glow.

As night descends, my thoughts take leave,
Dreams of mischief, they weave and weave.
In the quiet hour, I laugh and sigh,
What a ruckus, under this vast sky.

Gentle Breeze and Fleeting Thoughts

A gentle breeze, my frolicsome friend,
It tickles my nose, won't let me pretend.
Thoughts drift away like kites set free,
Could my worries be as light as a bee?

In the dappled sun, a silly thought,
What if grass whispered all it had bought?
Imaginations dance, oh what a spree,
A rabbit debates with a tall honey tree.

With each gust, I ponder a plot,
Could my garden gnome really tell me a lot?
He stands so still, with a grin and a stare,
Waiting for the moment to join in the air.

As shadows grow long, I snicker and beam,
Life's just a jester, or so it would seem.
In the breeze's embrace, I sit and I laugh,
What a marvelous tapestry each day can craft.

Lanterns of Reflection

Under the glow, I see my dear friend,
A moth dancing wildly, no need to pretend.
He flutters about, giving it a whirl,
Is that a dance or a messy twirl?

I ponder the meanings of shadows and lights,
Why do they frolic on cozy nights?
Where does the moon go when clouds intercede?
A game of hide and seek, indeed!

My lanterns are winking, holding a secret,
Do they giggle at me or make me regret?
I want to join in their whimsical play,
What mischief awaits at the end of the day?

In this bubble of giggles, I drift and I dream,
With lanterns of laughter, my heart's a stream.
I toast to the night, to all the delight,
What's better than laughter beneath starlight?

Where Stillness Breeds Contemplation

In the calm of the night, I stumble upon,
A heap of cushions, oh, what a con!
I sink in deep, lost in my thoughts,
Should I train pigeons to juggle or trot?

A cat by my side, with a pat and a purr,
Are we both lazy, or just a big blur?
She yawns wide, steals the best of the chair,
In our world of stillness, does she even care?

The stars giggle softly, they know my plight,
I ponder their secrets in the still of night.
Why can't I twinkle, like them so bright?
Or perhaps just a glimmer, a small guiding light?

As silence wraps round, chuckles abound,
In my thoughts, the funniest quirks can be found.
In stillness we ponder, from dusk until dawn,
Is life just a puzzle, or a big game of lawn?

The Heart's Whispering Cradle

In a chair that creaks with glee,
I rock and hum soft tunes for free.
The cat stares with a judgmental look,
As if I've misplaced every book.

The world outside, it spins and twirls,
But I've found treasure in my curls.
A squirrel dances a jig on the fence,
While I sip lemonade — it makes perfect sense!

Neighbors pass with an odd raised brow,
Wondering why I'm talking to a cow.
Oh, dear friend, you have much to learn,
That laughter hides where the heart can churn.

With chipped mugs and wild dreams afloat,
I keep each note from my wayward goat.
This blissful chaos is simply a treat,
And solitude? Well, it's simply sweet!

Wrapt in Gentle Shadows

A leaf falls like a clumsy dance,
I wave hello, caught in a trance.
The wind whispers jokes from afar,
Like 'Why did the crow sit on the car?'

In shadows that flicker, I chuckle and sigh,
Moths in a flurry, oh my how they fly!
As evening descends, the stars blink in jest,
While I test my balance on a wild bird's nest.

A picnic blanket draped on my toes,
Hoping it catches the crumbs that I throw.
The ants plot a revolution below,
While I sip tea in delightful flow.

So let them march with tiny parade,
I've got my snacks and a shade to trade.
And me in my corner, a joy to be found,
Where silliness reigns and rhythms astound!

Veils of Serenity Unfurled

In my haven of whispers, shadows play,
Voices of birds at the break of day.
A breeze passes by with a sneaky grin,
Ruffling my hair like it's a game to win.

The old clock ticks in a rhythm so odd,
If it could talk, it would surely nod.
Time is a trickster, laughs at the wall,
While I munch popcorn, waiting for a call.

A spider spins tales that drift in the air,
Reminding me gently that life can be rare.
I wave to the grass as it tickles my feet,
Building a kingdom where sunshine is sweet.

The chair squawks complaints of being reclined,
But I assure it, with snacks we're aligned.
In my fortress of laughter, snug as a bug,
I celebrate solitude with the finest of hugs!

Ruminating in Candlelight

In the glow of the wick, ideas ignite,
As I ponder what's wrong with my last bite.
The cookie crumbled in disarray,
It seems the chips forgot how to play!

Mismatched thoughts, like candles, they wane,
Swaying left, while my brain starts to strain.
The cat makes a leap, an acrobatic show,
As I giggle at shadows that dance to and fro.

The fridge is a monster that grumbles and groans,
It whispers, 'Join me in the land of the scones!'
But I'm lost in my thoughts of splendor and cheese,
Wishing for snacks that would float on the breeze.

Oh, peaceful night, you burble and brew,
With candles for company and humor to strew.
I close my eyes, watch the laughter take flight,
As midnight's embrace wraps me warm in its light!

Gossamer Threads of Thought

A cat named Whiskers thinks he's smart,
He ponders life in every part.
On sun-drenched steps he plots and schemes,
Chasing shadows, lost in dreams.

A squirrel debates with his reflection,
While plotting snacks with keen perfection.
He hoards his nuts, a secret stash,
With plans that always end in a crash.

The mailman waves, the dog barks back,
As birds compose their morning track.
Each honk and chirp, a comic play,
On the stage of another day.

Yet in this calm, the world tickles,
With laughter hiding in the sickles.
Life's silly dances, day in and out,
In the gentle hum of joy, no doubt.

Fragments of Yesterday's Remembrances

Grandpa's stories, always tall,
Of giant fish and dog gone small.
Each tale a twist, a chuckle shared,
In memories bright, no one is scared.

The rocking chair creaks with delight,
It sways with laughter, day and night.
Ghosts of giggles float in the air,
As friends reminisce without a care.

An aunt who swore she could bake bread,
Ended up baking a shoe instead.
With flour dusted on her nose,
Her kitchen chaos always glows.

With each mishap, a treasure found,
In silly moments, joy abounds.
A tapestry of laughter spun,
In these fragments, life's a pun.

Solace Under the Old Oak

Under the old tree, children play,
With giggles and squeals, they chase away.
A lemonade stand, a sticky mess,
Each dollar earned is pure success!

The swing set squeaks, a joyful tune,
While ants march on with their afternoon.
They carry crumbs with great intent,
In their small world, no time is spent.

A dog named Rufus snores away,
While dreaming of chasing the sun's rays.
He twitches and yips, a lovable chump,
Dreaming of chasing the mailman's jump.

As laughter bubbles like a brook,
Every simple moment, a heartfelt hook.
In nature's laughter, worries cease,
In shared silliness, we find peace.

Memories in a Gentle Breeze

The breeze whispers jokes from days of old,
Like tales of socks lost in the fold.
Each gust a giggle, a tickle in sound,
Tickling noses all around.

Picnic ants hold a parade near,
While plans for snacks are quite unclear.
A crumb flies high, a bold little dare,
Each bite shared with mischievous flair.

Friends debate who's really best,
In a game of who can make the best jest.
A laughing match, who has the thrill?
With punchlines delivered in hearty spill.

As the sun dips low, shadows grow long,
In moments captured, the heart is strong.
Life's gentle breeze carries laughter's tease,
In shared memories that aim to please.

Where Silence Dances with Time

In corners where quiet sits,
A chair creaks, and laughter flits.
A squirrel debates with a shoe,
Who knew a sunbeam could argue too?

Breezes tickle the robe on Miss Cat,
As she ponders where the moths are at.
Time winks like a sneaky chap,
While I sip my drink and nap.

A lonely sock whispers its tale,
Of daring escapes and a summer gale.
As shadows prance and do the jive,
In this dance of quiet, we feel alive.

Neighbors peek through their window blinds,
Curiosity's a disease of all kinds.
Who knew solitude could be this fun?
With laughs from shadows—let's keep it spun!

Echoes of a Fading Light

The fading glow begins to tease,
As fireflies stage a wild freeze.
A beetle plays hopscotch on the floor,
While I chuckle at the evening's score.

Crickets recite their nightly song,
In a concert where no one belongs.
Whispers of dust float along the air,
I'll bring the punch; you bring the flair!

An owl hoots with perplexity,
Feeling odd in this set of serenity.
Sort of like an awkward dance,
Where silence giggles at each chance.

The moon peeks in, quite extensive,
Gathering mischief, oh so intensive.
Let's toast to the antics of the night,
With echoes of laughter that take flight!

Reflections in a Still Glass

A still glass holds the evening's grin,
With ripples mocking all that's been.
A leaf that fell brings tales of fun,
Of tiny battles in the sun.

Mice plot their escape by moonlight,
While the fireflies dart and take flight.
The world reflects in giggles anew,
Through mischief shared by two or a few.

A whispering breeze becomes our friend,
As it carries tales that never end.
Bottled laughter shines in the dark,
With secrets waiting for a spark.

So here we clink our cups in jest,
While shadows dance, we are blessed.
In reflections, life's ever so sly,
Chasing each moment as days go by!

Beneath the Canopy of Stars

Under a quilt of twinkling dreams,
Frogs offer serenades and quirky themes.
Whispers of wonder float in the air,
As laughter bubbles without a care.

Crickets tap dance in froggie shoes,
While the moon plays tricks, it's a funny ruse.
A gopher jeers from a cozy hole,
Casting its shadow on a night so whole.

The stars are cheeky, winking bright,
Stitching stories with threads of light.
Mice gather round for a midnight feast,
Each crumb a treasure, they feel like beasts!

So we chuckle at nature's parade,
In stitches of joy, our worries fade.
Beneath the sky, those giggles ignite,
In the great waltz of a starry night!

Unraveling Dreams in Gentle Whispers

In the quiet nook where thoughts unwind,
A sock has lost its partner, never to find.
The cat stares hard, judging my plans,
While I sip my tea, dreaming of bands.

Breezes tease the curtains with a sly dance,
I laugh at old socks with their faded romance.
A mouse runs by, a daring little beast,
But I'm too busy chasing my culinary feast.

The clock ticks slowly; I hum a new tune,
Imagining wild parties under the moon.
My slippers, the stars of this quirky stage,
As I twirl around, quite lost in my age.

Outside the night plays its own goofy show,
With chirping crickets in a zany flow.
I tip my hat to the goofy breeze,
In this haven of laughter, my heart finds ease.

The Stillness Between the Heartbeats.

Time wobbles here, like jelly on a plate,
In this waiting room, I contemplate fate.
The clock grins wide, it knows all the jokes,
While I chat with shadows, pretending they're folks.

Sipping on coffee that tastes like regret,
My plants are my audience, my best buddies yet.
They nod knowingly, as I spill my woes,
Twisting and turning in fervent prose.

Outside, the world rushes past in a blur,
While giggles erupt from a wandering purr.
The universe chuckles; it's clearly amused,
At my tangled thoughts, so delightfully bruised.

I wear my slippers like a crown on my head,
And the cat rolls her eyes, wishing me dead.
But here in this stillness, I feel quite alright,
As I dance with my worries, into the night.

Whispers of the Quiet Evening

Candles flicker tales of their past lights,
As shadows dance gently, revealing old fights.
A spider is weaving a comical web,
While I'm here wondering what's left in the bread.

The chair creaks loudly, a voice from the past,
Reminding me gently that moments don't last.
But a laugh spills out, like a wild chasing cat,
As I forget my worries and just chat with my mat.

A breeze carries whispers, both soft and sly,
I wonder if the stars are up there to pry.
Each rustle outside giggles in delight,
As I ponder the secrets of the silly night.

In this cozy corner, I find my flow,
With musings of mischief and laughter on tow.
The world spins away, a curious ball,
While I keep on spinning with glee, after all.

Shadows Stretching on Weathered Wood

The sun yawns low, painting stories in gold,
   While I sit pondering tales yet untold.
A duck quacks loudly, demanding my glance,
   As shadows around me break into dance.

Old wood creaks beneath all my thoughts,
In this garden of wonders where silliness rots.
  A bug crawls by, wearing a tiny hat,
  And I wonder if he knows where he's at.

The fence sways gently, gossiping low,
'Did you hear that?', 'No, do tell, is it so?'
The lily pads giggle, the world's full of jest,
  As I stretch my legs and let humor fest.

  In this painted silence, I catch my breath,
With laughter at life, feeling lighter than flesh.
And as night unfolds, twisted tales take flight,
  In the glow of the dusk, everything feels right.

Cradled by the Evening Glow

Bugs buzzing dance around my head,
I swat them away, wishing for a bed.
A squirrel steals my snack with delight,
I laugh as he scampers out of sight.

The glow from the lamp casts a bright sphere,
My cat sulks nearby, looking severe.
She plots for my chip crumbs, sneaky and sly,
I just can't win this snack battle, oh my!

Neighbors argue about their hedges,
While I giggle and sip my cool ledges.
The breeze whispers secrets, I try to hear,
But it only brings laughter and a silly cheer!

As stars blink above, I wave at the moon,
Wonder if it's always been such a cartoon.
With laughter as my evening's grand score,
I bet I'll remember this, who could ask for more?

Embrace of the Night's Stillness

In the stillness, the crickets narrate,
Of absent-minded woes and a questionable fate.
A raccoon rummages through trash with flair,
I can't help but chuckle, he just doesn't care!

Under the stars, my thoughts start to roam,
Plotting my escape to a whimsical home.
I argue with shadows that dance on the wall,
"Can you produce snacks?" I bellow, "Not at all!"

The moonlight reveals my trusty old chair,
That squeaks and groans as if it has flair.
Each creak is a joke, a giggling retort,
In this mystical realm, I hold court!

I tripped on the cat, and she shoots me a glare,
As if to say, "Please, try to beware!"
In the embrace of the night, I grin wide,
For in this mad world, I wear the fun side.

Where Time Sits Unhurried

Time appears to have lost the plot,
As I sip lemonade and wonder a lot.
The flowers bend, nodding in tune,
Even the breeze seems to hum a loony rune.

A neighbor's dog barks like he's in charge,
While the cat rolls over, acting large.
Moments drift slow, like honey on toast,
What am I doing? Oh wait! I forgot!

My thoughts waltz and twirl like they've got flair,
With no care in the world, just free as air.
A gnome in the garden looks quite bemused,
I guess even he finds this moment fused!

Hiccups from laughter interrupt my chill,
And the sun sets slowly, oh what a thrill!
Time may dawdle, but I do not mind,
In this whimsical realm, pure joy I find.

Flickering Shadows of Memories

Shadows on the wall perform a ballet,
As I reminisce about the good old days.
A bird sings off-key from its hidden lair,
It must be my cousin, with musical flair!

I once lost a sock to a laundry thief,
It haunts my dreams, a bizarre motif.
Each flicker recalls a long-lost jest,
Where laughter reigned and we were simply blessed.

Stories of awkward dances and shoe-less nights,
Where mischief brewed under dim city lights.
I prepare for the memories to merge and collide,
In this tapestry of humor, I'll take them in stride.

So here in the night, my heart becomes light,
These flickering shadows dance with all their might.
Embracing the chaos of laughter and glee,
In the comfort of solitude, I choose to be free!

The Comfort of Unspoken Thoughts

In a corner, I sit with my drink,
The cat winks, as if it can think.
Shadows dance with tales untold,
While my mind wanders, a bus so bold.

A squirrel scuttles, stealing my snack,
I ponder if it's planning an attack.
Thoughts bubble up like soda on ice,
Why can't I get something nice for my slice?

I argue with ghosts of my past,
They laugh at my choices, a comical cast.
A breeze whispers secrets of days gone by,
I snicker at echoes, oh how they lie!

Yet, in silence, I find clarity's glow,
The loudest laughter is heard in the slow.
So I sip my drink, and chuckle anew,
In this jumbled mess, I find joy too!

Reflections in the Still Waters of Time

By the puddle, I sit with a grin,
Watching clouds compete, who'll win?
A frog leaps high, it's quite the show,
I muse 'bout life, why bother, though?

Time skips like stones, plop and splash,
Rickety weeds, they make quite a clash.
A dragonfly zooms, in a suit so grand,
I envy its style, oh, isn't it bland?

Birds gossip above in the sunny haze,
I join their chat, through a whimsical gaze.
They squawk about worms, the juicy delight,
If I had wings, oh what a flight!

Reflections ripple, laughter like sound,
In this silly moment, joy I have found.
I'll sip my ideas from this cool pool,
For life is a circus, and I'm the fool!

Sitting Still with My Thoughts

Nestled on steps with a goofy face,
The wind whips 'round at a curious pace.
Thoughts drift like leaves, swirly and wild,
Some make me chuckle, a peculiar child.

A beetle marches, with pomp and flair,
Does he ever stop to ponder 'who cares'?
I offer him snacks in a tiny defense,
He scuttles away, my kindness immense!

Memories visit, wearing silly hats,
They whisper 'remember that?' even to cats.
I laugh at their antics, the jests they bring,
Life's a circus, and oh, what a fling!

Sunlight dapples with humor quite bright,
In quiet moments, the soul takes flight.
So, I sit and smile, in my own little space,
In stillness, I find life's most wonderful grace!

Reverie Beneath the Open Sky

Beneath the blue, I stretch like a cat,
Clouds shaped like sandwiches, how about that?
I dream of picnics with giant desserts,
But ants are the uninvited guests in my shirts.

A ladybug lands with a noble intent,
I wonder if it's royalty, heaven-sent.
It shakes its spots, like a monarch crowned,
While I giggle softly at the sights all around.

The sun throws tantrums, hot on my nose,
"Hey, not too much – chill!" I suppose.
With laughter in pockets and hair in a mess,
I relish the breezes, life's sunny excess.

As twilight creeps in with a wink of delight,
I watch the stars play tag in the night.
So here I lounge, with dreams like a kite,
In this quirky reverie, everything feels right!

Caressed by Soft Sighs

With every creak, the old chair groans,
It's not just me; it's got its tones.
The wind whispers jokes in leafy tones,
While squirrels judge from their furry thrones.

A feather drifts and lands on my head,
Is nature trying to mess with my dread?
A bug buzzes by, like it knows what's said,
Here's to solitude; I'll sip on my bread.

The sun sets low, casting silly shadows,
A crabapple flops like it's dancing bravos.
I snicker at clouds dressed in rainbow halos,
Life's a circus, and I'm in no farrows.

So raise a glass to the quiet delight,
Where laughter and sighs play tag into night.
In this little realm where the odd takes flight,
Each giggle a tune, the heart feeling light.

Elysium at Dusk

As day's bright canvas starts to unwind,
I chase fireflies, leaving worries behind.
They flicker like wishes, so careless and blind,
In five-star flicks, all the world's poorly rhymed.

The garden gnomes snicker, they surely do see,
How grass tickles toes, and it's quite the spree.
A joke shared with weeds, oh lulled memory,
Peeking among blooms, wondering who's free.

The stars make an entrance, each one a prank,
With twinkling glances, no reason to thank.
I sit with their laughter, though sure I'm quite blank,
A celestial show, in glee I'll be drank.

So let the night wrap me in snickers and quips,
As dreams lead their dance on my whimsical trips.
Elysium whispers, with humorous tips,
Where silence is golden, but laughter just flips.

Where Thoughts Take Flight

In the gentle nod of a rocking chair,
My thoughts do a jig, without a care.
They flutter like butterflies; oh, beware!
One just landed here, in my wild hair.

A cat on the porch grooms with great pride,
Sighing at birds that won't let him slide.
He tosses us looks, like what's left inside,
While I hold my laughter, trying to hide.

The moon croons softly, a ballad for two,
Promising maybes, as laughter's the view.
Each blink tells a story, so charmingly new,
In this twilight garden, where dreams just flew.

With crickets composing a symphony bright,
I dance with my shadows, hearts bursting with light.
Here, thoughts take flight on humorous nights,
Where solitude sparkles; it's pure, such a sight!

A Cup of Echoed Silence

Pour me a cup filled with whispered delight,
A dash of chuckles, a pinch of moonlight.
Stir in some sighs, the mischievous bite,
And sip on the stillness; it feels just right.

A chair bows low, just waiting for more,
To cradle my thoughts as they dance on the floor.
The sun shares a wink, as shadows explore,
Echoed chuckles, it's laughter's great lore.

The hum of the crickets, the breeze giving chase,
The silence wears laughter, like a cheeky face.
Where moments collide in a velvety space,
I brew my own joy, in this quirky place.

So fill up your cup, let it overflow,
With tales from the night, and the secrets we know.
In echoed silences, the fun does grow,
A toast to the quiet, let the laughter flow!

www.ingramcontent.com/pod-product-compliance
Lightning Source LLC
Chambersburg PA
CBHW060142230426
43661CB00003B/533